To Bill
with love

Rumor

Collected Poems by

Silva Zanoyan Merjanian

copyright © 2015 by Silva Zanoyan Merjanian
First printing

First printing, March, 2015

All rights reserved.
Printed in the United States of America.
No part of this book may be reproduced
in any manner whatsoever without written
permission except in the case of brief quotations
embodied in critical essays and articles.

Cover lPainting by Suren Vosganian

Cover Artwork copyright © 2014 Noah's Ark Art Gallery

ISBN: 978-0-9960599-7-8

Library Of Congress Control Number: 2015935055

A COLD RIVER PUBLICATION

Cold River Press
11402 Francis Drive
Grass Valley, CA 95949

www.coldriverpress.com

Dedicated to
Ed, Vic and Michael Merjanian

Acknowledgement

My gratitude to family and friends, especially to my brother, Vahan Zanoyan. Heartfelt thanks to members of Blackwater and Follow the Muse poetry groups for their love and support. Special thanks to Dr. Bedros Afeyan, a physicist, writer, sculptor and painter, for his mentorship and guidance. Very grateful to Noah's Ark Art Gallery for the use of the book cover artwork, by Armenian painter, Suren Vosganian.

Table of Contents

Rumor	13
We the Women	14
Another Place Another Time	16
Saints in My Rain	18
Perspective	20
Muse	21
Rooftop	22
Tonight	23
Doves of Beirut	24
Awakening	26
September	27
My Slivered Lebanon	28
Rain	30
Under My Skin	31
Tale of Fathers	32
Collateral Damage	34
Ninety Eight Springs	36
Refugee	38
Beirut	40
Sentimental	43
The Bath	44
Destined	46
Mea Culpa	48
In Vino Veritas	50
Falling	51
City Trees	52
Hesitation	54
La Femme	56
Till Death Do Us Part	58
Tell Me About Your Father	60
Bluebird	62
The Call	64

Table of Contents

Clothesline...65
Growing Wounds...66
Blue Collar...68
Between Rosary Beads..69
Borrowed Sugar Borrowed Time..70
Room Service..72
Choices..74
Suicide...76
Tears Know Not a Crocodile...78
Motherland..80
Ritual...82
The Irishman...84
Twilight Zone..86
Trapped...88
Poets in a Pub...89
Radiating Debate..90
Where the Truth Is Strewn...91
And Such It Was...92
Between the Sheets...94
Almost...96
Lived Well...97
Exile..98
Spring..100
Distance...102
Now and Then..103
Home...104
Nostalgia...106
There's No Turning Back...108
Converge...110
Woman..111
Author's Bio..113
Publication Credits..115

Rumor

Collected Poems by

Silva Zanoyan Merjanian

RUMOR

A dyspeptic shadow on highways
in my pockets sweaty fingerprints
assurances, blue inked lint

no rooster's crow in these streets
only in deep sleep one clutched to chest
spreading tacit rumors at dawn
of October rain's euphony
raising nostalgia in dry heaves
tremor of promises under four inch heels

dull end of tongues grating truth
in lukewarm baths
maimed fox-tailed backseat drivers
washcloth in hand
veins licked raw on extended necks
nights, slurping myopic gods diurnal grins

I, in narcotic cities immune to mockery or praise
in smell of damp pews, dreams hostage
you, a rumor in euphony of rain

May 31, 2014

WE THE WOMEN

We hold our liqueur 'tween our teeth
celebrate sisterhood as spit and swear
see our moistened pitted tongues
flick and flatter in daylight
pregnant magnets spinning in flight

we lift and probe with glances, crawl through skin
lipsticked kisses bubble and pop in hazed air
to sink in pinks and luscious reds over raised glasses
acid traces bend bright cherry umbrellas
to hide glare of spiced faces and timid- praise grins

we measure power in galloping breasts
enhanced, reduced, stretched, rounded, supported, bare
they wobble and trounce miles before our voices hound
to hold between our legs knowing smiles
gathered from each others lashed raw backs

we bring our mines to blessed hills with severed sights
flirt within our lips drawn thin over stringed *faux pas*
we lie in crinoline holding the devil hostage intrauterine
smoldering alone until rivalry rings grow dim
while we kegel our resolve in stories misty and grim

kiss kiss, let's do this again soon
a lizard licks the last drop of sun off my skin

June 12, 2013

ANOTHER PLACE ANOTHER TIME

Which side should I have turned a face
gleaming in doubt's pant and sweat
subtle the beauty of disgrace
when bare and humbled yet not slain

had I known might of absence
as I knew weight of a presence
are we strangers foes or friends
are we past the sniff and scratch
weary of a race
chasing tails not attached

I have a splinter for a rib
another made of Deir ez-Zor sand
pressed a palm on dunes that used to breathe
had I not risen from each grave
with bite and grace all in place
had I not known putrescent waste
such will and strength would not have grown
such love I could not have left alone

with each shave of embalmed grin
undertaker's hand off my skin
scorn of time, to be born again
and sense you in a parallel path
were you the hunter with remorse
blowing on feathers lying still in hand
a wound revealed
I thought not mine, except I felt the pain

come now, meet my eyes over flickering lives
I am where what seems, almost never is
and what's seems not most certainly is
spiked truth rolls down green hills
I catch its lint on such thirst
modified values
autopsied lives
knowing nothing of pride
on conveyer belts gliding backwards
I reach for flame retardant loves
while etching dark poetry in your palm

publish if you can this night
in its flaring nostrils scented oil
it holds words that feed the beast
you named daylight
where I was left behind

another grave
another time

December 9, 2013

SAINTS IN MY RAIN

I learned the rain in cursive slants
I learned lying on doubts
spread on the sacred and not
spread on my bed, my pillow, my exhale
the crust of every lie I loved
tainted with silver sliver of your tongue

I turned that night on its back
after you went to bed
your streets indebted
to shadows of restless dreams
bruising on its replaced ribs
where trash collectors compress
disposed remnants
in the ruble
life's severed limbs
an envy here
a longing there
a nothingness holier than my prayers

and I add
that face without the lips
under the face with muffled shame
under the face I used to have
on heaps of unfinished poems
where a lemon tree and jasmine blossoms
promised mornings
colored and scented at my fingertips

I learned the rain in every lie
in stammer of your pavements
where Saints gather in line at rock bottoms stacked
between my howl and a crow's black squawk
wrists dripping prayers on St Rita's solemn face
she sympathizes but says tonight she owns the ledge

there's always mad laughter at the foot of beds
where Saints sleep on their sides facing the drapes
that catch the city's quieting breath
misting under street lamps
that catch impelled compromise
in bourbon shots and blues on a clarinet
as lonely as you
that time when you asked my name
sometimes I tell you
long after you've gone to bed

October 27, 2014

PERSPECTIVE

Deference distended on contrails
corrosion of clouds nailed on sightline
opaque with gratitude scrapings
grease of childhood handprints
colorless placidity unhinged
reticent nights balance on a kiss
that never was
but promised more than any yet held
on lucid tongues

she stirs decisions in syncopated rhythms
rehearsed and rephrased on tea leaves
outgrows his wingspan most mornings
in time for murder of irascible crows
on daylight's yawn
to peck on leftover significance
at yesterday's pedestals

May 12, 2014

MUSE

She's in between poems you wrote in your sleep
between madness and euphoria in your dreams

she's between lips brushing her breath's skin
between fingerprints you kissed on your sheets

she's between moans of the night and sunrise
between notes of Beethoven rolling down your tongue

she's between tuned strings of a cellist
on canvas in between shades of sunflowers and iris

she's laughter, snagged between your metronome beats
she's in between an ocean and a sky on its knees

you're between paper and a drop of ink

February 13, 2013

ROOFTOP

I die at dusk every day
on a rooftop in a city with no name
daughters unborn to me mourn
in bruised nights' wombs
voices I do not recognize
utter prayers to deaf trees
shaking my limbs off their leaves

a city breathing heavy with its sins
buries me in its alleys
smell of jasmine and urine on its walls
where once I cut a vein and emptied
time's venom under blinking neon lights

there's no distance to my pain

I'm born at dawn every day
in a sac of daylight
with an appetite to eat moments in slow bites
roll them on a dry tongue
linger on the sweet and bitter
oozing from each tick tock shortening my life

I can't remember where I loved you in between

it is dusk again,
I look for the rooftop
I hung my fresh laundry on

June 9, 2013

TONIGHT

Tonight a thousand eyelids will close on beautiful lies
and quivering lips will sleep unkissed
untouched by sultry blue jazz in the dark

tonight lust will blister on menopausal gritty tongues
and blind vultures will circle parameters of a man's heart

tonight middle aged men will look for love in midtown bars
and women selling artificial flavors to the tune of hallelujahs
will sharpen their knives

tonight poets will find the words to color their hell
and dip their pens in wounds that aren't even theirs

tonight somewhere it will rain on wingless birds
their love songs mending broken pillows in high notes

tonight she will step out with her hair down, in new stilettos
she'll blow a kiss with naked lips through the door left ajar

tonight, tonight's no different than any other night
the walls are thin, the moon is skinned, blindfolds handed free

May 18, 2013

DOVES OF BEIRUT

Doves were arrogant in those days
feral, territorial of ledges
I hadn't snapped their necks yet
through grind of metal
on bone, stone
through air sharpened on greed hones
no scream left in punctured lungs
fate duct-taped to fetal nights
barricaded behind shadowed ribs
that hardly rose for a fight
underneath rubble of lord's prayer and adhan

they pecked at concrete
heads bobbing, waiting
waiting
they knew I'd come
they knew I'd tire of walking
your curved dead-end streets

I knew those ledges well
gravel and loose feathers
wet with rain
stuck with white droppings
to my young toes curled on grit

but I knew your streets below better
lick of diesel on asphalt
grief's iron reek in gutters rising
damp alleys breathing
breathing
the way the old do
those who'd seen the blade
cut through flesh

a sigh every third inhale
a pause before funneling
jasmine and mold laced gasps
into patched veins
tied to the stone
tied to throbbing ground
with historical claims
to the sea breeze
that couldn't cool their burns
still rummaging for life
as they used to remember it

I walked on sweat of fig trees
on your sidewalks bleeding at cracks
when you had the pigeon for dinner
and I starving, gnawed on bones
where I'd tied my message
pleading for your unclutched claws
on my debt

I hear you like your whores younger these days
and you rather have your sons as killers
blind and foaming revenge at mouth
darbouka between their knees dropped for guns

streets mapped in bite marks
on time I served now dyed ash blond
I look away
the way the old do
eyes on the distance to your bleeding ledge

March 25, 2014

AWAKENING

Simplicity with which morning casts aside a venal night
no aurorean regrets, but hushed readings
where words stretch a paper-cut in thin air

color-blind wolves retreat
and she catches a glimpse of her self in their eyes

all that spills on night's curves and corners now half dry sticky mire
on eyelashes sharpened behind muslin lies
artless restraints rust
the light catches their decay in glorious colors

she's startled by her voice that sounded different in the dark
was that her in a ring throwing gloveless punches and missing every sneer
she comes out with less skin, unlearned fear dripping down a broken crown

years stand rolled into haystacks in a field of mined hindsight
virga of decisions fail to clear a path
but every welt now a blue vein on cupped hands
where she holds a voice that edited the night of its flaws
what pushes against her ribs also pulls a smile on morning lips

she finally fits in her skin although thin at places
and still as crazy as the bird that keeps flying into the window pane

at peace, in the morning that slaps the night when no one's looking
walks in with a wink and a dance with no backward steps

September 20, 2013

SEPTEMBER

September's the new lover in my bed
we snort new lies and hold, in sweet breath
till eyes accustom to the dark
and scent of potpourri is lost between us

September is my summer matured
into a harlequin *mélange* of elegies

it's my sleepwalk to the street-lamp 'round midnight
in a city that loves smell of the rain in my hair
and there's the man under its hazy floodlight
with a 3 day scruff, grinding a cigarette
he promises is his last

I tell him I love him and I mean it for a while

September's inure to absence of you
now svelte femme fatale flirting winter
or second fiddle to a protagonist
it depends on parried questions of the day

September breathes in your gaping mouth
but don't hold it to its promises
they're idle rain on rooftops

September 3, 2013

MY SLIVERED LEBANON

She remembers fragments
broken in thin lights
city suspended in delicate lies
lounging gods, bouncing tranquil shores
golden rays, stories dancing on limestone
where Pigeon's Rock once kissed azure waters
and settled in drunk faithfulness

oh how a flirtatious moon
loved spread of silvery thighs on shimmering sea
oblivious drum-beats spilling from yachts
and lovers' locked gaze heaving under moss-covered walls
stolen kisses rising in giggles to envious skies
caught in olive trees, lining French named streets

but she whispers in shadows of her nights
of another time
when biblical cedars bowed in others' blood
and clouds wept salted Mediterranean prayers
sanguine vines on alabaster legs
held balconies by one iron thread
terror on tongues wet with warm milk
brought mothers to their knees
doves on rooftops flying in circles
witnessed vultures pecking at cadavers
smell of burning flesh
feel of red shrapnel
sound of explosions
ferment only in her head
yet still deafen thunders
and blind grieving Shapash

she whispers in shadows of her nights
of another time
where once Anath feasted on figs and dates
licked honey off her fingers
rolled ethnic bulging dice
dashing hope and ashes wide

Shapash – Phoenician goddess of sea
Anath – Phoenician goddess of love and war

March 8, 2013

RAIN

Rain has never washed a stain
or a conversation at 2 am
yet it never fails to pick
the little dust on street lamps
give them legs to crawl down posts
smear in black, mud in your thoughts

it's only when you close your eyes
behind shades that dim a flight
a Riverdance on rooftops
it sounds clean and cleansing
all the streets that twist and squeeze
new exits now swirl in mind
and here you are still standing
behind haze of an oblique drench
carefully choosing the words
that you know will break your teeth

no, rain never washed a stain
yet you wait for its scented dance
to wash plight of a burnt night

August 19, 2013

UNDER MY SKIN

My pen thrust under Gordian ribs
you bled in pigments of melancholy
on Egyptian cotton
thread count in verses of lament

you lay on piles of edit

silence under my skin

rain was merciless that year
digging you from every landfill

you, in jazz of ebrious nights
you, on lips insipid leftover wine

absence rising to crescendo
your name slavers on repining spring

silence prises terete sighs
I wake a poem slipping through cracks
in quiver of fingers I once kissed

March 28, 2014

TALE OF FATHERS

Days roll on each other
evenings descend
absorb seams of growing years
cooling horizons inflamed
with fever of a man's dream

brightening glow
of spark 'round his mouth
still burns her mind
puckered lips bartering nicotine
to numb ache of fate
squeezing his lungs

she remembers squint of his eyes
through smoke whirling
rising to edge of his world
leaving him cross legged
god- bound, mystic
away from reach

she built bridges in that smoke
to cross to his world
her breath fogging his shadow
that never fell on hers

time, razor sharp
cuts a scar of thousand bridges
suspended in smoke
falling on new ones built on a headstone

February 10, 2013

COLLATERAL DAMAGE

Morning arrives charred
served on a disassembled night
its curled edges, ashes on waking eyes
no smoke in sight, no trace
where old mistakes aspirate donated lungs
burked storms under soft pillows
plump with the geese not the feather

as if a night could not satiate viscera of dreams with its cant
as if doubt drains into power pipelines as tear ducts dry
and conscience blazes in defiance fueled bonfires

had you not heard panting in medicated doldrums of their minds
had their stuttered remorse turned the soft soil of tomorrow
had you not loved only to stay alive
morning would have arrived perky and bright
and you too would have heard the finch outside
instead of the crackling of the fire

August 28, 2010

NINETY EIGHT SPRINGS

April skies,
covert layers
in pale blue

she's drawn

weight
of mass graves
shackled
on her tongue

she stretches
digs
into cerulean

scratches past
dressed skin
ninety eight
springless blue

under fingernails
brown blood
air on air
spread tasteless
over Deir ez-Zor sand
shifting, burning
heaps of bones

her eyes
deny their hands
stained
with Armenian blood
scrubbing a black sky
never to pale blue

April 24, 2013
98th anniversary of Armenian Genocide

REFUGEE

Outside, desert air licks tents with an icy tongue
creeping under pegs unto the sand floor
where she waits morning, legs squeezed, trembling tight
her mother's warm breath with a hint of onion and lentil smell
brushes on her face, calms tremor of awake nightmares
her sister's knees dig into small of her back

she tucks her cold feet under her aunt's ample buttocks
finds comfort and safety in the call of unwashed bodies
familiar, earthy, sweat of family in deep disturbed sleep
on worn beige mattresses pressed side by side

a limb resting on her distended bladder feels heavy
she knows she has to hold it in, till light leaks
from between clouds bearing down, birthing morning relief
over a tense night battling more than a winter's wrath

it is not safe to walk at night to the makeshift bathroom outside
her father had said, not even holding mother's hand
she remembers the stars as they faded one by one with each thrust
when strange men tore into her that night, their moans mocking whimpers
escaping through large fingers pressing on her mouth

she feels the sting first, between her bruised thighs
before the wet warmth soaks through her pink pajamas
darkening with yellow and red princess patterns
into the coarse mattress, where her siblings lie
entangled in fading dreams of home

She couldn't hold, she is after all only eight years old

April 8, 2013

BEIRUT

Over there
all that happened
(and didn't happen)
folded
packed in mental mothballs
stories fading with licked creases
some reduced and softer versions

wonder why I preserve breaths
forced through my lungs in those days
stringed around the eye of a hurricane
circling, demonic, nameless
shaking me shameless for a day

on nights when a collective sigh stings
and I can't tell
which tale will toll for me
and which nocturnal howl
will lift the dust
through endless times
relive slivers
on a pink tip of my tongue
afraid to bite a dreamt memory
that it might hemorrhage
bleed the night

I want a dripping whiff of that afternoon coffee
instinctively bitter, solemnity and hot
ten minutes when lonely hearts
willed an arching cease fire
and time hovered among us
long enough for my mother
to build castles in my cup

over there
the man flying his doves
on the roof across two streets
remains a blur
but the doves stirring the air
in perfect shades of unison
(I had named them after heroes long forgot)
sometimes still raise dust in my room
of their feathers' aches and plight

I believed then
I could break away
would break away

I did one day
the doves were left to die

over there
at dusk my father played the mandolin
and my mother's voice filled all the gaps
between our breaths -
the dam that held surpluses of war
long enough for us to shed in dreams

continued on next page

BEIRUT
continued

       why do I long for hell
       on nights
       when I can't sieve my sigh from the wind's eye
       and I wonder if I ever broke away
       from a circle named dead doves
       perhaps
       scent of jasmine
       still smells like home
       back home in the rain

                         May 15, 2013

SENTIMENTAL

November calms restless swallows
as they leave me
a *mise en scène* in air

night's cool breath, jazz purling
on fogged windows
eases panic of empty beds

scent of serein
cradles memories
I had wrapped in kisses
dried between poems

November morning, notes on lips
to lyrics lost in blue feathers
I dip a biscotto in my coffee
raise my hand with élan
and wait

November 8, 2013

THE BATH

1.

Descent into scented moisture
time-splash etching marble
candlelight winces in wary flickers
night's cold jagged edges crumble

artificial warmth of an iron-clad tub
fogs lavender soaked memories on wet thighs
sloughed skin floats with forgotten unshed tears
laughter that didn't make it to hopeful lips
unassembled thoughts, sighs furled in armors

weave of a sultry voice through steam
glistens on parted lips
(she too must have loved and lied, lied and loved)
trickle of rain through maze
of dust on window-panes
grabs streetlights' reflection by the waist
slow dances blemished hand-made shadows
down the seal into guarded solitude

the night macerates in cooling water
swirling around the drain
a spider spirals down from the surface
struggling against the flow
clutching traces of a child

2.

a child
once seated on a low stool
in a small room off a kitchen
suds collecting 'round the drain
on a cracked concrete floor
pot of water on a kerosene burner in the corner
gentle hands lathering laurel and olive oil soap
pouring water from a dried carved gourd
over unruly curls clinging to unfortified eyelashes
rubbing against a white apron
stained with tomato sauce, smelling of mint
oregano, all spice, comfort, home
where sadness could not linger
for longer than one could hold a breath.

January 18, 2014

DESTINED

I am afraid to fall asleep
without a dream
where every qualm and allegation
on garrulous nights' hirsute back
dissipates in your bruised palms
remedies for wind's foul breath

I am afraid you'd be enough
measured in gulps
of sweet bitter taste
yet in dawn's benign light
I'd be a pest on gossamers
on window's edge
losing its fragile breath

I am afraid of rain's quiet flow
beyond trellises of bougainvillea
beyond wave of black shawls
on greenest lawns
and the pastor's solemn grace
and up on a hill a lone wolf's howl
will reach my heart in perfect rhyme
and sound as if it were my name
as I scribble yours on quilted lid
salt of your hands on my blue lips
I am afraid to fall asleep

June 3, 2014

MEA CULPA

Fall has not yet licked the sky
against my palm the evening
damp with California dreaming
wide eyed
perched on live wire
I found my place
ancient yet not
here
not here
this not that
nothing defined
yet no cowering shadows
no doubt plastered on tongues

but clean slates don't come without cracks
ink dries in carmine on sins and wings
dropped in collection baskets not aired

déjà vu dripping through fingers I dipped
twice in pleas slippery on churned confessions
friction burns, skid marks on longings
barefoot on ravens lining the streets
croaks pecking silence of baring trees
I wrung my words
I fled the scene

he said never return to where you were traded
for plucked feathers
till spring when pails are sieved
of bones and carrion flowers
and he finds your fear in California dreaming
skipping on an ocean's skin
then melt
melt
and mold on lips you want to kiss

October 30, 2013

IN VINO VERITAS

In debauchery one nostril flared
fulcrum tip at a sparrow's head
mirada ignored
alight on a solo dance

a dare, a missed step, a blushing fall sans grace

come morning
dry tongue smoldered to a name
murmured past midnight
on salted lies, sediments of magnum wine
a buzz in a draft
maudlin *solitas* on one side of a four poster bed

tango of words used to suffice
but for the duende of a night
soaked in jasmine and French lyrics
rising with a tremor between strings of a Spanish guitar

April 4, 2014

FALLING

In rind of wishes sticky on lips
and sermons' echo on facepsalms slipping
in envies squirted on spruce and cedar
whims twirling, spiraled, speckled
gossamer visions of friendships withered
in crevices of an upbeat mien
Your name hidden in prayer embers
I mend among buds of poems
flying on a trapeze
with no one at the other end

December 25, 2013

CITY TREES

Gazers in perpetual grey
mute canopies lick facades' pallid mores
camouflage ennui on rod iron railings

branches with decorum
graze balconies where women
in desiccated ardor sunbath bare chests
leaves catching sighs on Gitanes smoke
never mock baltering sway of their breasts

shading tram-stops and kiosks
on the *qui vive* for raconteurs on benches
where old men sit and covet firm *derrières*
reminiscing when they had them on their knees

trees prime camaraderie at *café trottoirs*
in pastel shades before jealousies taint
afternoon lattes in bitter hues of dull beige

they catch the drizzling spit of a city's malaise
twigs pressed against windows
watch us on our yellow bedspread
old grime and aches washed in spring rain
new leaves recover god's name
and yours in familiar whispers
rustle them to me as I in blushed kilig
crown you king

May 3, 2014

HESITATION

Have you seen this autumn sway
flirt the corner two blocks that way
where September waits
to cross a light
to cross a fear
a rattling thought
too bold
too bold
for a girl still green in cadence of mid-winter hail

have you seen the sidewalk sweat
with nostalgia for summer's scent
bare skin and a dare
tease of first raindrop in my hair

swallows scrape fall's first fragrance
in a city hardly damp
women chew and spit feathers
stretched on beds
empty under a man's weight
familiar smell of preserved bloom
nails retracted
oh but ever tightening on throats of those who once loved them
convenience, chewable berry flavored keeping all tamed

have you seen me
folding corners of my skin over a gash
sting of fall sweat dripping
from pupils dilated with verses I read
the burn I hide under my tongue with your plump name
roll it out on certain nights
on buyer's-remorse stuffed mattress
I let the silverfish scurry guilty
desperate for a space between baseboards
like I, once between your thoughts

have you seen sway of autumn on white sheets
I spread over three summers
chipping at corners peace colored paint

September 17, 2014

LA FEMME

Some say he'd gone mad in early May
pacing weary torturous nights
in his white shirt sleeves rolled up
stained with days of sweat and paint
lusting for the perfect woman in his mind
she called him to the blank canvas's throb
to his paints and blunt mixing knife

he dipped his brush in crimson red
painted a pulse that could only beat for his crazed eyes
gold in her hair blazed on his canvas
dim light caught the sparkle in her blue eyes
he painted her luscious lips with his bourbon drenched mouth
his brush stroked her curves to fit perfectly in his arms

trill of her laughter on his Gitanes yellowed fingertips
he brushed her spirit in colors of spring

dawn squeezed through rain - washed panes
crept on the floor and cast
a transparent linen on his broken body
his paint-brush dug deep in his heart
footprints in his colors on the ground
of a perfect woman gone feral outside his mind
a blank canvas torn to shreds

a pale moon lingered in May skies

May 4, 2013

TILL DEATH DO US PART

She became the space between his thoughts
resonating in the downpour of fall rain

he
her trophy, bound in fraying lace
she vowed to serve 'till death do us part'
polished it dry

traces of him still in old picture frames
strong chin, clear features pressed against cold glass
the rest of him left with her
in faded shades of a sunset painting
hanging on their composite mantle

they became the pause before sunrise colors the alleys

the rest of him rattled her brittle bones
and she sucked on marrow of his at hairline fractures
carnivorous
she flossed his deep laugh from her veneers
spit a chewed spleen
as he regurgitated forgiveness

layers of them
now sloughed skin on sharp turns
loose change between lust cushions
filled with wet olive branches

they walked the streets
thinking the slopes will forgive
the way they sliced a liver
molted distinct voices in one note
rode the late night sarcasm
muffled labor pain of a breeched 'us'
moaning confessions next to a picture frame
fogged with nostalgia's halitosis

they walked the streets
thinking a night won't gnaw on their cannibalized remains
on which she raises a leg daily,
on which condensed drops of who he was once
catch the morning light

October 23, 2014

TELL ME ABOUT YOUR FATHER

He crossed his legs at ankles
tweed trousers hem caught life
in one hour loose fragments
above sprinkles of course hair
he leaned back notepad in lap
twirling a Bic pen between his bony fingers

tell me about your father he said

my tongue found the chip on my front tooth
I had gnawed on tip of a Bic pen once
slouched over homework on a Sunday afternoon
pelt of rain on window panes
silencing my father's presence in the room

tell me about your father

outside Geneva *bise* minced the silence
white lace curtains on French doors let Lake Leman
glisten a halo above his balding crown
my father too had lost his hair
but his brother died with a full head of black curls
after his return from Siberian exile
mother made sure we stayed quiet
and out of his way in those days

tell me about your father

the grandfather clock on the wall obtruded
into my insight, I waited for the bird
to announce end of our session
it had startled me once when I had gone inwards
to untangle words clenched on vocal cords

dit moi de votre père

my father spoke four languages
language was not the barrier

there was a faint smell of soap in the room
I wondered if it was his cologne
my father used Old Spice
I could not remember if only on Sundays

ah bien, when you are ready

I leaned forward wanting to catch a memory of that scent

February 3, 2014

BLUEBIRD
A night with Bukowski

I invited him one summer night
come I said, let's sit in bed

I, with a glass of wine
his voice, unorganized in my mind
he, on the right side
eyes fidgeting with something in the air
perhaps a memory from a nameless night
with a nameless older woman offering a worthy rump

his voice trailed
over our affection for urban scene
smog
concrete
gutter irrigated life

he was flicking his cigarette ashes from my hair
when I mumbled, *oh do tell, how to walk through the fire*
outside, a city quieted down
he leaned into me and said, *you don't need much babe*
all you have to do is make it out there

he talked, I listened
I talked, he dozed off
I let him
(it didn't end well for the fat one who didn't)
till the cricket on the eight floor balcony started to show off
(we were friends on lonely nights)
he threw a slipper at it
it reminded him of poetry readings he said

my glass empty now
(he drank from the bottle)
lulled in illusion of intimacy in soft bedside light
I did it
I let my bluebird out
don't kill it now he said
don't kill it babe
just don't share it except with the night

his breath got heavy on my neck
but I could tell his mind was on his whores
this then he said
this then is all…

a depressed night pushed itself in
from the open balcony door
old man, it said, *she can't follow*
she's not sure of anything
neither am I anymore

by 3am the cows called him home
I turned off the lights
spooned the sound asleep city outside
and wished for a cricket on my balcony floor

May 10, 2013

THE CALL

A voice slides down my stretched neck
curves 'round the nape

and I'm back
in smoldering August
standing at the window
long after the city turned off its lights
watching the woman
in a white *combinaison*

she leans down a window
cooling off the walls
with a bucket of water

unexpected breeze teases
loose strands of her hair
beads of perspiration
vanish in swell of her breasts
she raises her damp face to the *frôlement*
they could have been lovers
for decades
hint of a smile pulls on her lips
as it moves swiftly
to the couple
making love on the balcony
above her window
behind red geraniums on the rail

a voice tousles my undone hair

June 14, 2013

CLOTHESLINE

White bed-sheet flaps stories
crisp, flirtatious, free-style dance
a breeze intimate with its creases
searches musky scent of better days
billowing with slight hesitation
it tells, regrets, retreats, few secrets kept

clothespins pinch where memories fade
sunlight softens few tear stains
clumsily mended late night spats
cornered kisses, promises shred
damp, scratched, raw night tales

it waves against green shutters
dead geraniums catch peeled paint
squeak of rusted hinges
over swoosh of stories sliding
clutching frayed cotton fibers
clap of breeze against blush of cheeks

a breeze bored and out of breath
slaps, caresses, coaxes, pleads
remains tethered to dead-end romance
clothesline sags where white bed-sheets dance

March 17, 2013

GROWING WOUNDS

Only on the underside of rain
voices fall as prayers on moist imperfections
I wake as fragile as dawn's teeth- less grin
here the night forgives age of tears shed in dreams
for every punch without exclamation mark
for every drop of flattery induced wrong

it took a certain kind of man to ask me to talk
pass the words through rays and see them as pearls
he wanted to sleep and wake on my lips
but I was curled under a detached left arm stroking my raw spine
while right hand flossed my blood from hyena's fangs
fed its starving ego leathery confessions- slathered praise
who knew they spewed poems from Laundromats, mismatched
exchanged quotes at luncheons, cannibalized conscience
waiting for dusk to prowl for hungry poets whoring for a belly scratch

I could only be on the underside of rain
here the city is gentle and graffiti's genuine
and the white flag I wave through bars on shadows
as I watch in a distance the jungle and pagan dance
and hear subtle mockery under roar and rage
grows at every sunset without the white smoke
I long for smell of green grass in the fall
and the sound of my confirmation name
not knowing a hatchet nor how to bury one in cement

I drown my father's voice when he shook his head and said
hush now child there is no underside to rain
yet it's the only place I can keep my wounds honest

August 24, 2014

BLUE COLLAR

Life sewn at seams with coffee break daydreams
embellished memories, cardboard box stored
pressed, flattened, futile-weight blessed fate

smell of mildew on regrets creeping in speeches
heartily delivered on Sunday fast food dinners

blame burnt black, gargled in salt, spat at capitalism
'round every sour life event

a town asleep to drone of machines real and imagined
caught in its bolts, spasm of dreams
fading between dusty numb fingertips
scratching snores, once heaves between sheets

sound of failure drowning in beer burps
and blue light of late night television talk shows
self-pity chewed and forgotten in pockets of over-worn jeans
more comfortable with every wash and rinse.

January 14, 2014

BETWEEN ROSARY BEADS

Umbilical cords twisted' round forged sins
birthing canals holy water rinsed clean
pushed into virgin hands hauling contempt
white robes, bloodied crucifix, murderous saints

wombs, bones, conscience, dusted evening prayers
what dried in milk ducts, echoes on stone walls
induced shame weaved in seven sacraments
in the name of the father, and the son
and the holy spirit innocence shoveled

June 7, 2014

BORROWED SUGAR BORROWED TIME

Sunshine scrapes rust of rod iron railings
shimmers cobwebs on balcony plants
and what doesn't spill on cobblestones below
streams through open windows
stretches on waking bare limbs
dries dreamless nights' last drop of sweat
dewy stance poised on threshold of consciousness

a Mediterranean sky absorbs the city's vibrant colors
scent of the sea in blooming trees, in sun kissed hair
on young girls' skin glazed with a hint of *Bain de Soleil*
home as sweet and safe as God's lure of heaven

street vendor's voice calling price of peaches
insulate the morning a familiar soft hue
rituals of coffee and idle gossip trill
the humid air in narrow alleys
radios blare love songs through shutters
on yellow walled buildings
diffused in city noise and coo of doves on ledges
they fade in wall crevices storing a city's secrets

bounce of gold crosses between breasts
colorful hijabs 'round others' bare face
friendships seeded in borrowed sugar, borrowed time
she, unaware of borrowed wailers on their way
makes plans on a sunny balcony as she hangs
her blue jeans on a clothesline
moments before war drums ripple through crisp calm

June 20, 2013

ROOM SERVICE

Daylight squints through heavy drapes
you, stretched on last vacation day
twirl painted toes at edge of bed
wondering who lay in this spot
before you and before them
and why hotel sheets are always white

waiting for room service to knock
wheel in a continental for a thousandth time
and wheel out nights in stringed origami
unraveled wallpaper in eleven-twenty-five

a door slams shut in the hallway
a carry-on checking out
perhaps it's the middle aged man
seated across the dining room yesterday
a bleached smile, a receding crown
a stiff neck twisted 'round frequent flyer miles
later footsteps and his aftershave
trail after you to the eleventh floor
and disappear with a briefcase
behind a Do Not Disturb sign
hanging at an angle on his life

perfect palm trees on a beach
framed in blue sky, washed -out calm
blend in the room, there, yet not there
together with mini bar tales
lies, laughs, deals and tears of them all
where housekeeping wipes last trail
of who you are and every thought
fingerprints dusted off your breath

they're not us, no we're not them
but who pulled same covers over their heads
powdered skeletons in a bed
memories mingled in laundry piles

you pack to take back home
all dared, presumed
risked, measured and tipped
caught in draft of rotating doors
except what you leave behind
in steam of shower and pillow talk
and the number on a room

August 17, 2013

CHOICES

Come back to bed he said

it was August heat
Bach's cello
and a blue moonlight
at 2 am

ceiling fan swept the air
spread yesterday's dust in the dim light
my skin damp with his sweat
I watched a night heave outside

a full moon cast stripes
through plantation shutters
on memories of you on swollen lips
(that tasted salty at 2 am)
down my bare breasts
extended on the wall
on to a floor unsteady under my legs

come back to bed he said

it was time
I knew

I let go of you
we had broken skin with words
bridges long dissolved in choices
I had waited at your door too long

I let go of you
just like that

untied myself
from you

I left moonlight stripes with the night
and joined him in pitch dark.

May 1, 2013

SUICIDE

We danced once
when all one could hear
was rise and fall of people's dreams in REM
a cricket's elegy lost in the evening's scent
laughter from life's junkyard he recycled
in turgid nights with spasms of a gritty hunger

somewhere, rustle of thighs falling sideways
on lies and knives and snap of knees
closing on promise of truffles in warm mud
calmed a laugh, scraped a lie off my tongue

he drowned his in travesty and drugs

we danced
he in his polished shoes
I in bare feet on red tipped toes
reaching almost rim of his mind
burn of strings in dark henna lurching night licked
to a pale blue in my eyes
his, tightened around his neck, he finally smiled

we danced in his cupped hands
in spittle of poems writ past midnight
in intact fragile shells
till dawn's nosebleed dripped
on gilt rooftops, bird bones
and cannon's breath
I tasted morning on his lips
before we wore name tags in a stampede
lost the music to a final bow in death's standing ovation

I hear the applause fading alone on a stage
wearing a laugh too big for my face
tucked behind measured steps
sliding
sliding

August 12, 2014

TEARS KNOW NOT A CROCODILE

Written, mere froth on light, missing special effects
lariated tears deserve another look in poets hands
misery's sap meandering through fragile eyelashes
lines warped deluged in disposable anodyne

yet flowing inwards, a raspy song converts
a road taking another name at sharp turns
tears change to throbs that keep a night awake
restrain a river's ache wiped dry of self -respect
glass chewed on gums bleeding blue in lyrics

dampen a pillow before daylight cracks an egg
till you lose (your) taste in strong coffee and strong men
remember through squints spasms you once chased

tears in clichés sliding at corners in folded verses
yet you can't skin them from your pen ejaculating laments
when there's no one listening but half deaf nocturnal voyeurs
unblinking, unimpressed in flatulent pompous feathers

April 10, 2014

MOTHERLAND

Strain of heritage, serrated
bent at waist
light breaks through me
in colors bled deep
through soil of this motherland

I whisper to the twilight
I am not a daughter
not with these blue eyes
nor my wild curls catching fire

I straighten
spill your pain
rancid in my veins
look, I shed you in layers
wrapped in double helix
around my vision

I took off your clothes
and walked naked into the ocean
you, dry seaweed
holding on to my bruised fingernails

I set my sons free while still in womb
kissed their soft heels on their path at seventeen
daughters were not born to me
I whispered to them anyway
you are free
you are free

mountains shiver in echo of your centuries
bouncing on a thousand church stones
but I am no more wrapped in your fury nor your ache
only in a yearning I don't understand

June 29, 2013

RITUAL

The day drops on tile floors
moments in glass marbles
scatter 'round bare feet
some lived into scratches
some shine without my prints

they levitate into beads of rain
on a 'wind' shield
I wipe them
with one exhale

daylight dissipates
toes dipped in self-loath

embrace the night
a scent of solitude on my skin
soaks one pea drop at a time
lavender cream runs a tingle
through my veins
I am on pause
repose

now
now I can look straight
into my mother's eyes
I untangle my eyelashes from hers
I wash the crusted salt off hers
I wash the shield of mascara off mine

I carry weight of her death
under my eyelids
squinting at her memory in them
I chant the rhythm of guilt with no words

till she closes those eyes I can't stand

what's left is a nightingale
her song shrouds my sleep

May 2013

THE IRISHMAN

There's a sadness in Irish eyes
harboring comfort in anguish
thousands years in the making
a secret code in their laughter
'round incessant toasts
macerating in Celtic rain

chagrin in steel blue eyes
dusted with late night dry sighs
burden of fathers hauled
from calloused hands of their fathers
and theirs
drool of life bartenders wipe
off their counters in local pubs

and courage in Irish veins flows
as Liffey gurgles its Viking source
on grey damp mornings
as death daunts and scandals
emerge from humid stones

love of country and family
rouse the lymphatic Dublin night
and an Irishman in moonlit melancholy
grief squeezing his pen's throat
rattles cage of fate and more

September 26, 2014

TWILIGHT ZONE

There is a place with portals to an alternate timeline
surrender, and the nice man taps a vein
sings a song
pushes synthetic assurances
through a plastic tube
brines your brain in unconscious bliss

wait for it
wait for it
now turn the lights out
there will be time to drool a grateful smile

walking in a labyrinth
too many dead-ends
mixed messages oscillating
inverted

knock on a door with a blinking 'Dare and Truth'
people playing musical chairs with fake tunes
you know you'll always be the first to go
when chairs are dandelions on which you blew

you pucker your lips for an adieu
get a Glasgow kiss on your third eye
right when conga drums get louder and louder
jump off the pendulum
let go
feel the rose petals under your bare toes

a wine glass appears in your hand
you toast a dead poet still writing dirty letters
around the corner Hurst is playing Sparrows
and Cohen seducing without any effort
dance me with a blindfold on your eyes
you say *yes please yes but just for a moment*

focus, don't get caught in bong of a bell
yes that's a sunflower field at the far end
and two boys running around in circles
which reminds you the piano has to be tuned

another corner and there's your muse
where have you been you almost scream
but she's calling your name and it's getting clearer
and the nice man is smiling too close to your lips

all you want to ask him is if truth's overrated
instead you whisper *how did it go?*
he says you were brave
he says your name twice again
then a third time
still reading it on a plastic red wrist-band

October 25, 2013

TRAPPED

I lived for a while on skin of a poem
afraid to press my lips to its flesh
I lived on tip of a slipping tongue
lest it might disturb all who dreamt

city's damp concrete was kind to me
it's the silence of crows in winter fields
grating the madness inside me

not dressed to run, not dressed to stay
trapped in the moment
between a scream and a laugh

December 28, 2013

POETS IN A PUB

Pints of beer link our troubles in broken chain
lips on brims speckled with words we chase asleep
cigarette-breaks coil conversations around a floating spool
ever dripping with rain caught as stylus in a groove

and a river turns in its sleep and mutters a song

he keeps his promise to take you to Rockforest bar
names drag and drop but life's rhymes and meter thrive
the bartender shakes your hand with a look in his eye
and you can tell he knows
he knows you think of what you lost every night

a river turns in its sleep and mutters your song

August 26, 2013

RADIATING DEBATE

Dinner was always fish on Fridays
he insisted on fresh caught and gutted
while he waited with a Starbucks coffee in hand

a ritual on the Pacific Coast pier
where for years men bonded in such traditions
and debated the issues
stock market, prostates, women
as the old fisherman they've known for decades
wrapped for each catch of the day

nowadays she insists on chicken
some friends still hang out at the pier
they argue on levels of radiation
from Fukushima disaster
and stare at the Pacific
as they would at an old friend
dying of cancer

January 4, 2014

WHERE THE TRUTH IS STREWN

On the road to old city of Van
(where Armenia once rose)
in proximity of a 'slowdown
children crossing' sign
my jaw bone protrudes
from gravel and dust
sadistic hatred still serves
caravan of shallow mass graves
my papa's skull cracked
his pleas convulsing stones
to spare his little girl

no dirge or mourners
nor mercy to cover
my pubescent limbs
my headstone's but a scream
etched with blood and tears
waking your docile night

here lies your conscience
packed in a scimitar sheath
where there is a 'slowdown
children crossing' sign
in weeping killing fields
where truth strewn
slows to a stop

January 26, 2014

AND SUCH IT WAS

A *pas de deux* in mist rising
above warm pavements in October rain
light splashing in its scent
names murmured again and again
raveled in linens, vows
and smell of youth in sweat

a taste held too long on naive lips
amuse bouche for bitter tingle in coming years
she could not love in pastel shades
nor in cheeks flushed in butterfly lies
it was blood on lips and growls
it was spit and poetry scratched eyes

sarcasm crept in her push-up bra
while girls who knew not flavor of 2 am
flirted in brown eyes cast down
their touch hardly a wisp of a child's breath
here now, gone then
in his blue bulging crotch
silver-plated testicles
paid for, restored except for rhythm and bounce

such love could not breathe in her peripheral view
blinking charred scars on ambivalent skies
his name she utters sometimes
when a percipient night
blots spill of irony on time

and such was love
not tamed, not spent
reduced to a glow slanting in eyes

December 14, 2014

BETWEEN THE SHEETS

Us
Us
A few bread crumbs from a toast
Us
Glow in the dark risqué thoughts
Bach
Last night
Light from the bathroom past midnight
Socks
Laughter of two little boys
Dr Seuss
Two pairs of feet between ours
Tickles, giggles
Sundays
Sound of rain on skylight
Cuddles
A few squabbles and silence
Us
Just us
Coffee and toast with a note
4am
Snores
Snores
Pillow talk
He said then she said
They were both wrong

The piano men
Smell of fresh laundry and lavender
Nights implacable and long
Heating pad
Neruda
Flannel
Moisturized skin
A book, two books
Jazz
Secrets
Secrets
Voice of an angel in my head
An arm I'll stay wrapped around
Mornings arriving early
Me alone
Poems half written and done
Poems between toes and toast
'Round Midnight and Monk
Nostalgia
Right reasons
Brave decisions
Thoughts that glow in the light
Just love
Always, in absence of rats and such
Fresh sheets and I
Between over and under

November 3, 2013

ALMOST

Are you happy he'd ask
pulling me to him
how can I not be I'd say
this is heaven
here
with you

watching the *Jet d'Eau* from our terrace
shoot up 140 feet in the air
rain down in thousands
of shimmering diamonds on Lake Leman

some forever caught in clasped eyelashes

what would a beautiful lake know
of what I left behind
walked out with a suitcase
his ring on my finger led

Rive Gauche lights, colorful fishnets
glistened on the bank
caught in guilt, fresh writhing wet
the lake remained stolid

are you happy he'd ask
I would kiss him, *yes, yes*

carefully circling the edge

May 20, 2014

LIVED WELL

He watches them dance in a haze
last of his wine in his hand
frayed life remnants in his pen
they dance for him
those who bled him
those he drained

fingers quiver on tattooed names
'till he finds their arched backs
feels their teeth on his lower lip
tastes his name on eager tongues
they dance for him at 4 am

his eyes narrow for their faces
but all he sees is a poem in each curve
confabulates a shriveled night
uttering *sans pudeur*
dance my loves dance
rip this estranged night

July 20, 2013

EXILE

To my grandfather

Iron curtain raised its hemline and news trickled
bloodied, scabbed with uncertainty, blackened
they said there was a knock on the door at 4 am
they said a house stood void of breath next day

credulous dawn spread quietly in Etchmiadzin's narrow streets
playful on rooflines, damp on bird wings folding dreams
some did not see July morning burst in lovers song and dance
fragile fingers crushing profanity enforced prayers
on panic and urine soiled floors in dark crowded cargo trains

grind of wheels on railroad tracks sealed a fate
scraped memory of soft soil under the plum tree
your shirts still hanging on clothesline tied to its branch
last colors of summer breeze fading on worn faces
stench of human waste in pails thrown inside with loafs of stale bread
lungs exhaling putrid promise of homeland
reduced to cattle, grateful for meager humanity, rationed

your breath frozen on thin panes countless nights leaned against
crippled, unable to meet your blank stare
silence inside broke into shards of ice at daylight
hemorrhaged guilt on artistic slander hands
tailoring in vain a road map back home in your head
reading the wind in braille, hearing it whimper like a sick dog
you stopped looking for cranes on rooftops
head on pillows stiff with blame, suppressed longings, hindsight

six deported for manual labor, only five outlived Stalin, pardoned
they said they put your bones to rest in an unmarked grave
they say Siberia still groans under your ache's heavy weight

October 8, 2014

SPRING

On days like this
light carries sultry swirls to her fingertips
as if a summer night biting on a breeze
spring raindrops plump with promise
hit heaving ground
burst into half conceived laughter
steam in her eyes

reality gently peeled
nail scratches inside her skin
she slides through tight ribs
eyes on *joie de vivre* threading clouds

whispers color lips in rose scented pink
half truths or lies

on days like this
she'll wear her blue dress
she'll leave the curls in her hair
red toenails scratch inside your skin
as you try to escape your daydreams

she won't look back again
crushed apple seeds under her heels

March 3, 2013

DISTANCE

Sober sighs ransomed from insomniacs
counting their loot of hours spread on blues

jeremiad wisps fan this unopened night
nocturnal birds' song, deliquescent carnage on dry ink

it is late, I should sleep, but it's all wrong
like a righteous chorus I remember in the cork

I edit what's not in print, I add a black dress to the skin
of the distance between these hours that catch the spit

October 21, 2014

NOW AND THEN

I know how it sounds when it stops raining
musky smell of soil clings to the sough
combing with wet fingers vulnerable leaves
separating eyelashes from flutter of fantasies
gauzy on a lingering blush

indifferent to taste of blood on raw palate
lashed with proper speech
no sense of belonging between thighs crossed
no tremble with stimuli to your voice
a verse hovers ditching every line
undone pixel by pixel
sometimes I miss that lilt
sometimes I cringe at what I've loved

October 21, 2014

HOME

Words on an epicure's tongue
that subtle bitter
lost on an audience
handpicked from chorus lines
while I savored buoyant questions
to the edge of your mind
knowing there will be no answers
in suburbs graveled white

but on this night
the universe is crawling
on skin soft with expectation
and I have untied silk rhymes
lifting the bluebird's cleavage
you might as well have caged it
between your colored doubts

are you listening at this moment
or are you asleep spooning spines
bent where you have dotted

all I ask is for hail in December
charting my hiding
sanding raised eyebrows
I will lie in your embrace
and deal with the aftertaste
at first crack of dawn
in absence of verse hygiene
graffiti clinging to your sunken chest
because the universe is crawling
on skin soft with expectation
and I am lost in a blizzard
that resembles your voice

you see there is no one at home
and home is everywhere
in the vast distance
in memories' dead weight
in winter's renewal act
in promise of my eyes
and in your empty palms
where I pressed my face
fearing my many names
but one I left on rooftops

November 28, 2014

NOSTALGIA

This calm has rocked the evening
to forgetfulness
it is peaceful
when nothing's remembered
but strength of my hands
quiet of tongue pressed on your name
where blood clots
where jazz once flowed
jagged through veins

peaceful dead-end

till instinct bites the flame
and there's that want again
for the forest dark and dense
city skyline wet with rain
soft breeze subtly uprooting mornings
daylight that remembers me
undone
unmarked

dusk smells like I imagine you would
of possibility
I could do with, I could do without
it's the damn night that's still damp
where your poetry licked lips touched
when every star knew you were not meant
to hold a night like this and I
leaning against a dying vine

November 13, 2014

THERE'S NO TURNING BACK

*You live like this, sheltered, in adelicate world,
and you believe you are living. Then you read a book,
or you a take a trip, and you discover that you are not
living, that you are hibernating.*

Anais Nin

Can she come back
untouched
from this dance
to the end of each dream
having died again
between dissociations
comme il faut crushing
old metatarsals
and layers of malleable spirit
when heaven spread like a tablecloth
on indiscretions

you drew the curtains open
let the city in on your nightmare
where you saw her wide eyed, awake
dressed to tango
splinters from the wood floor
still on her bare words

sheets bruising
but no apologies yet
she's tasted sweat of a dream
and it's not of regret
but salt of a love song
in dim lit jazz clubs
smelling of cheap wine
streets of Havana
warm with the sultry rasp

she's tasted sweat of a dream
lips soaked in a poet's verse
mending with his voice
smoke from Parisian chimneys
on an autumn evening
as the rain falls

and when Lisboa calls
to Fado's heartache
there's no turning back
from night's naked air
having loved fearless
outliving yearnings
but for curve of a smile
she can't kiss awake

she blames him for that

January 9, 2015

CONVERGE

It is lonely on cool tiles of my corruption
eye on domes of Rome, midday stretches
lethargic silence on ashes I burn
in the high sun on red rooftops basking in refuge

feathers from ashes, feathers short of a wing
to glide down like a raven to your chiral streets

there's a congregation praying for my salvation
a choir singing the gospel, mirage on church steeples
I wring last drop of resolve in your mouth
and keep a river in my womb to wash my disillusionment

squatting to gut irony collected on your stairways
raw against my breastbone stringed on a fishing line
putrescent promises familiar in flared nostrils
same as ancient prayers filtering from parched tourist lips

I will tell you again of pagan sins kneeling in confession
when you stop searching for the righteous woman
buried under four layers of leathered skin
you ask me if I want to pray with you for redemption
I ask you where do we go from here
where do we go not to converge in a dream

February, 27, 2015

WOMAN

Dusk will come and go
you know how it is
with fire bitten sunsets
seepage from elbows
yesterday's scabrous lust
familiarity suds
popping in kitchen sinks

ask me about 2 am
if I'll still be painting
bulbul's intimate song
on your dry chipped lips
palm catching
your nightmarish murmurs
curls caught in your Ophelian streak

January 31, 2015

Silva Zanoyan Merjanian is a widely published poet who grew up in Beirut, Lebanon. She moved to Geneva during the Lebanese civil war after personally experiencing the devastation of her beloved country. She later settled in California to raise her two sons with her husband. Her poetry reflects a little of what she took with her from each city she lived in. The nostalgia for her roots, her Armenian heritage, her deep sense of humanity reduced and elevated at the same time in life's events, permeate through her poems. Her work is featured in anthologies and international poetry journals. Actress/Producer Eabha Rose recently read four of her poems; *Choices, Rooftop, Doves of Beirut* and *Suicide* which gained international acclaim. Her first volume of poetry, *Uncoil a Night*, was released in 2013. You may contact her at silvamerjanian@gmail.com.

Publication Credits

The Literary Groong: *Muse, Spring, Refugee, Ninety Eight Springs, Beirut*
Mad Swirl: *Lived Well, Rooftop, Poets in a Pub, Sentimental, Falling*
Poet's Basement at Counterpunch: *Tonight, Beirut, Refugee*
The Oddity: *Borrowed Sugar Borrowed Time* *
The Oddball Magazine: *Where the Truth is Strewn*
Red Fez: *My Slivered Lebanon*
Young Men's Perspective Volume 3: *Collateral Damage, Rooftop, Tonight, Till Death Do Us Part*
Munyori Literary Journal: *Beirut, We the Women, Mea Culpa, September, Where the Truth Is Strewn*
Ygdrasil, a Journal of the Poetic Arts: *Blue-Collar, Mea Culpa, Awakening*
The Original Van Goghs Ear Anthology: *Doves of Beirut*
The Knot Magazine: *Under My Skin, Happiness, In Vino Veritas, Suicide*
Ginosko: *Clotheline, Tonight, We the Women*
San Diego Poetry Annual: *Perspective*
San Pedro River Review: *Tell Me About Your Father*
Blue Max Review 2013 & 2014: *We the Women, Destined*
The Art of Being Human, Vol 3, 6 &12: *Clothesline, Muse, Choices, The Call, Bluebird*
The Inspired Heart Edition 1 &2: *La Femme, Ritual, Borrowed Sugar Borrowed Time*
Songs For Julia, by Julia Priest: *We the Women, Tonight, Rain, September, Till Death Do US Part, Another Place Another Time, Falling*
Away Fly Words, Poems for Fukushima: *Radiating Debate*
Resonance: *The Bath*

* This is an edit of the original featured there titled "Sons"

Silva Merjanian's second collection is a lush, full-bodied zinfandel infused throughout with the terroir of her Armenian heritage. These poems are deeply colored with currant and cherry, rich with tobacco and licorice, meant to be rolled around the tongue, and exhaled with a peppery finish.

        Phillip Larrea, author of *We the People, Our Patch*

Silva's poetry rewards the reader with the gift of exquisite lacework, adorned with choice words and skillfully wrought poetic imagery, which allow you to get a glimpse of both the intoxicating sensuality of survival and the scalpel scars on the frail skin of life. Many-layered, it excels alike in depicting the sphere of personal experience and of traumatic social issues.

        Dr. Aprilia Zank, *Lecturer for Creative Writing and Translation Theory–Ludwig Maximilian University, Munich, Germany*

Silva Merjanian continues her journey into poetry with this new collection. Her voice now takes us deeper into the shadows and hurt lockers of the heart and soul. A rawness calls out from these poems for an answer to the human condition. Meaningful and rewarding for the reader who will swim in their waves.

        Brendan McCormack, *one of the most unique voices in contemporary Irish Poetry; author of Phuckle and Selling Heaven*